PACIFIC COAST HIGHWAY

A Photographic Journey

TEXT: **Bill Harris**

CAPTIONS: **Fleur Robertson**

DESIGNED BY: **Teddy Hartshorn**

EDITORIAL: **Gill Waugh**

PRODUCTION: **Ruth Arthur and David Proffit**

DIRECTOR OF PRODUCTION: **Gerald Hughes**

CLB 2675
© 1991 Colour Library Books Ltd., Godalming, Surrey, England.
All rights reserved.
This 1991 edition published by Crescent Books,
distributed by Outlet Book Company, Inc., a Random House Company,
225 Park Avenue South, New York, New York 10003.
Color separations by Tien Wah Press (PTE) Ltd.
Printed and bound in Singapore.
ISBN 0 517 06027 2
8 7 6 5 4 3 2 1

PACIFIC COAST HIGHWAY

A Photographic Journey

Text by
BILL HARRIS

CRESCENT BOOKS
NEW YORK

A few decades ago, when resort hotels began springing up at the southern tip of Baja California, the paved highway ended at Ensenada, more than eight hundred miles to the north. The airplane made their properties accessible, but the hotel owners began agitating to have the road extended. The Mexican Government didn't seem too interested and one of the hotel men blamed his competitors up north. "The highway will never be built," he said. "Why? Because the state of Baja is more powerful politically than this territory. Tijuana would become a ghost town. Nobody would stop there except for gas. They'd never let that happen."

But never is a long, long time. The road was finished all the way down to the tip of Cabo San Lucas in 1973, and the wilderness the Mexicans call La Peninsula California and the Americans call Baja was open for business for the first time. The gas stations at Tijuana had a lot to celebrate, but rather than becoming a ghost town the city got a new lease of life.

It isn't that Tijuana wasn't lively to begin with. From the day it was founded in 1903, it was one of the lustiest cities in all the Americas, a mecca for sailors and marines stationed in Southern California looking for something a bit more exotic, as well as ordinary tourists and Californians looking for bargain shopping and Mexican food untainted by Texas influences. All of that still lures visitors south of the border, but when the government tourist office began an advertising campaign with the theme "Mexico Offers More," it might have had Tijuana in mind. Far from a tacky border town, it's a bustling little city bursting with a surprising elegance. It has two arenas for bullfights, but it also has a country club and a golf course as American as Scotch on the rocks. Its downtown shopping area has its share of souvenir shops, but it also has high-quality crafts shops and branches of the finest specialty stores from every part of Mexico. It offers jai alai, but the locals are more passionate about baseball. And the new Caliente race track, which features both thoroughbred horses and greyhounds, thoughtfully provides a gas station just in case a potential visitor might have thought the only reason to go to Tijuana is to "fill 'er up."

Credit for Tijuana's transformation clearly belongs to the highway, which the Mexican Government has designated Route One. But it has brought other benefits, too. It makes it possible to drive all the way from the tip of Baja to the top of the Olympic Peninsula, a distance of some 2,500 miles, with the Pacific Ocean on your left nearly all the way. Interstate Route 101 follows the coast from Los Angeles to Olympic National Park, but in California the scenic route is the Pacific Coast Highway, Route One, from Capistrano Beach almost to the Oregon border. The combination of the two roads is nothing short of spectacular. More than just ocean vistas, it is a trip through beautiful mountains and valleys, charming towns and bustling cities, and an excursion into the fascinating history of the Pacific Coast.

THE SAN DIEGO COAST

Most Americans consider San Diego a Navy town, but the fact is that the Navy didn't put down roots there until World War II. And though it was the biggest and most important base in the Pacific theater during the war years, it became a shadow of its former self after V-J Day. The Navy is still there, but there are more retired naval people in San Diego than men and women on active duty. An important reason for the latter is the seventy-five-mile coastline from the Mexican border to San Clemente.

It begins in the south at Imperial Beach, one of California's best-kept secrets a short distance from the border crossing at San Ysidro. Along with the other towns along the Silver Strand, the beach is becoming more popular than ever, especially among young people. For generations of Japanese-Americans, though, the oceanfront strip has been more important for growing celery than for surfing, fishing and building sand castles, even though it is only eight miles from the resort that has been attracting the rich and famous for more than a century, the Hotel Del Coronado.

Across San Diego Bay the string of little communities from Ocean Beach to La Jolla are loosely connected by a boardwalk overlooking wide beaches. Each community has its own personality, but to outsiders they represent every cliché about Southern California. There are surfers on the sand and rollerskaters on the boardwalk, bodybuilders flex their muscles and very serious bicyclists hide behind dark glasses and toss offended looks in the direction of runners who get in their way. It goes without saying they're mostly young, or at least pretend to be, and all of them have rich, dark tans. La Jolla, whose name means "the jewel," is within the San Diego city limits, but it has its own post office and people who live there in Mediterranean-style mansions and watch their gardeners tend masses of flowers at the edge of the cliffs much prefer you to think otherwise.

The gardens of La Jolla are arguably among the best in California, but it's not a good idea to pick the flowers. A few miles north, on the other hand, there are fields of flowers at Encinitas that were meant for picking, though only by the commercial growers who planted them. Buy a bouquet almost anywhere in America, and chances are good that at least some of the blossoms burst into bloom along the San Diego County Coast. The county's northwest corner is the huge Marine Corps base at Camp Pendleton, which extends for almost thirty miles along the shore.

THE AMERICAN RIVIERA

Orange County wasn't named for the color of gold, but it might have been. It wasn't named for its golden sunshine, but it might have been. The almost eternal sunshine makes it beautiful and it takes lots of gold to live there, but the name comes from the fact that before the subdividers arrived on the scene, it had the biggest concentration of orange groves in the state.

There are people living there today who remember them, and who remember when the oceanfront was described as barren, in spite of the brilliant blue ocean it overlooks. Among them is former president Richard Nixon, who was born at Yorba Linda in the county's northeast corner and established his home away from the White House at San Clemente, in the county's southwest corner.

San Clemente was one of the earliest real estate developments in Southern California, built in 1925 and boasting that each and every one of its white stucco houses with red tile roofs had an unobstructed view of the sea. The view also includes, as regular as clockwork every year on March 19, the return of the swallows to the mission of San Juan Capistrano from their winter vacation in South America.

The mission is said to be haunted by the ghost of an eighteenth-century Franciscan friar. If it's true, he probably can't believe his eyes. The landscape has completely changed since Disneyland first opened its gates in 1955, and though progress hasn't changed the natural beauty of the coast, it isn't because developers haven't tried. It was an inspiration to artists who flocked to Laguna Beach at the turn of the century, and to Los Angelenos who discovered Newport Beach when a streetcar line was established between the two cities at about the same time. Then, in the 1960s, long after the trolleys had stopped running, young people began to notice the surf running at Huntington Beach and the entire Orange County Coast, which was already known as the American Riviera, became the surfing capital of America, a title that is in some dispute, though not to those guys out there on the beach staring out to sea.

LOS ANGELES

In the early days of radio, comedians knew they could milk a sure-fire laugh with a joke about the Los Angeles city limits. But if the city is a monument to urban sprawl, its western border is fixed along a seventy-five-mile stretch of coastline between Long Beach and Malibu. And, surprisingly, in spite of industrialization and development, there are still stretches of unspoiled coastline within easy distance of downtown.

Even Long Beach, the seventh busiest seaport in the United States, takes a welcoming bow in the direction of funseekers as the last resting place of the luxury liner *Queen Mary*, and the world's largest airplane, Howard Hughes's *Spruce Goose*, not to mention daily excursions to Santa Catalina Island, a paradise twenty-two miles out at sea.

But the best seascapes are along the Palos Verdes peninsula, with high cliffs and deep, rocky coves and expensive suburban neighborhoods overlooking the Pacific. A little further north, the stretch known as South Bay is where surfing was first introduced to the mainland from Hawaii, and young people are still rediscovering its thrills. And beyond the Santa Monica Mountains is what may be the best-known stretch of beachfront in America – Malibu.

Many of the little communities along the Los Angeles Coast have been resorts since the middle of the last century, but Malibu is a late bloomer. The twenty-seven-mile stretch between the mountains and the sea became the ranch of Fred H. Rindge in 1892. When he died in 1905, his widow, May, began a fight to keep it isolated. She built high fences, patrolled by armed guards. She plowed up the existing roads and turned her hogs loose on construction crews sent in to rebuild them. When they were able to succeed, she dynamited their handiwork. The little war lasted until 1929, when the State, determined to push the coast highway across her land, took the case all the way to the United States Supreme Court, where May lost her last battle. She also lost nearly a million dollars a year fighting her long fight and was forced to sell not only the right-of-way for the highway, but her valuable beachfront property as well. The land was bought by movie stars, the only ones who could afford it in those Depression years, who built elegant houses there, and as if to confirm whose side they were on in the battle for the Pacific Coast Highway, they built them with their backs turned to the road.

As impressive as their houses may be, their neighbor, J. Paul Getty, upstaged them all with the museum he created in the hills above Malibu. It was built in 1974, but except for modifications dictated by modern building codes, it is a faithful reproduction of the Roman Villa of the Papyri at Herculaneum, destroyed by the eruption of Mount Vesuvius in A.D. 79. The museum is one of California's best, but the building is breathtaking all by itself.

Going from the sublime to the ridiculous, when a huge boulder fell across the highway near Malibu a few years ago, a private citizen offered to remove it and then proceeded to have it carved into a likeness of John Wayne, which he placed in his yard.

THE SPANISH COAST

Beyond the Santa Ynez Mountains, the million-plus acres of unspoiled inland territory is Los Padres National Forest, a protected watershed named for the Spanish friars who brought civilization here in the 1780s. Their heritage is reflected all over California, but this stretch of the coast, that includes the city that grew around the Santa Barbara Mission and and extends north to the Spanish-influenced Hearst Castle, is still like a bit of Spain in North America. Even the climate made the Spaniards feel at home.

The highway follows the route of El Camino Real, the road that connected the original missions. But without modern road-building techniques, the missionaries were forced to skirt the mountains over the tidal plain and had to plan their travel to coincide with low tide. Those who had to wait for the ebb had time to contemplate the eight islands rising up from the mist in Santa Barbara Channel. Five of them became Channel Islands National Park in 1980, but most of its visitors, like the Spanish who preceded them, conjure up dreams about them from the shore at Ventura.

Santa Barbara faces south, and the protection of the offshore islands makes it the calmest stretch of the California Coast. But if surfers turn their noses up at it, they are the only ones. Its mission, tenth in the string running north from San Diego, is the most beautiful of all twenty-one of them, and the city complements it perfectly. It was no accident. After a 1925 earthquake leveled most of its buildings, town planners rose to the occasion and created a monument to Spanish Renaissance architecture that is possibly the most charming city in all of California.

The Coast Highway winds northward from Santa Barbara into the Lompoc Valley, where poppies and nasturtiums, marigolds and delphinium are grown for their seeds, and where the flowers that produce them present a dazzling display of color. North of the valley, bleak sand dunes rise as high as 450 feet, and by the time the highway reaches San Luis Obispo the terrain has become mountainous and looks like a perfect setting for a Western movie, which it has often been.

SAN SIMEON

The cliffs overlooking deserted beaches at San Simeon have hardly changed since Portuguese whalers made it their base a century ago. But up there on top of La Cuesta Encantada, the enchanted hill, is Hearst Castle, which its builder, William Randolph Hearst, called La Casa Grande. "Grand" is a puny word to describe it. An army of workmen labored from 1919 until Hearst died in 1951 to build the twin-towered castle with its three luxurious guest houses and formal Italian Renaissance gardens, and some portions of the building are still not finished. It was a deliberate attempt to impress, and it doesn't fail.

MONTEREY

The section of Route One from San Simeon to Carmel was the result of nearly thirty years effort by a doctor who was forced to make his house calls on foot and on horseback over the hills and canyons of the Santa Lucia Mountains. At first he envisioned it as a private enterprise, and after years of planning and surveying he estimated that he could build it for about $50,000. He began a fundraising campaign among the coastal farmers and ranchers, but when the collections came up short, he took his case to the State Legislature and work was finally begun in 1920. It turned out that original estimate was far off the mark. Even using cheap convict labor, the final cost was $10 million and the road wasn't finished for eighteen years. What they got for their time and money was one of the most beautiful stretches of road anywhere in America, winding through the mountains with breathtaking views of the sea along the way.

But there is a side trip that almost makes it pale by comparison: the 17-Mile Drive from Carmel Bay to Pacific Grove. If you happen to live there, your chauffeur can get you past the gate without paying the fee, but if you don't, its worth every penny. Most of the mansions were built in the 1920s and were clearly intended for the super rich. Its developers thought of everything, including a plant to wash and dry the sand on the beaches. But the main attraction is the Monterey cypress trees which grow only on the peninsula's southern shore. Robert Louis Stevenson once described them as "like ghosts fleeing before the wind," and the streamers of yellow moss clinging to their gnarled branches make it a perfect description. A lone cypress at Midway Point is the trademark of the Pebble Beach Golf Club and is among the most photographed trees in America. But be careful who sees your slides. The club claims that its image belongs to them alone.

Another inspiring side trip from the highway is the roller coaster-like Coast Road over the Santa Lucia Mountains behind Big Sur. It's narrow, it isn't paved and it winds along narrow cliff sides, but the views of the ocean and the mountains will make you forget that your palms are sweating. The road begins near the Bixby Creek Bridge, one of the most famous and spectacular bridges on the coast, which carries Route One across a deep chasm high above the surf.

Big Sur was a hot spot in the 1960s, when young people flocked there to sit at the feet of novelist Henry Miller. When the revolution seemed to be over, the Establishment moved in and the price of real estate soared. The same thing happened up the coast at Carmel, but the timetable was different. Before the First World War, writers such as Sinclair Lewis and Lincoln Steffans joined photographer Ansel Adams and poet Robinson Jeffers to find inspiration there. But years later, John Steinbeck noted ruefully that even he couldn't afford to live in Carmel. He preferred Monterey anyway, and the city today has reminders of him at every turn from Cannery Row to the Grapes of Wrath Antique Store.

THE PENINSULA

Even without having taken a course is cartography it's easy to see on a map that San Francisco stands at the tip of a peninsula bordered by the ocean and San Francisco Bay. But to natives of the area, "The Peninsula" is the suburbs, and it is further broken down into Coastside and Bayside. The former is a rather desolate, if not dramatic, place and the latter a rather heavily populated string of small cities including Palo Alto, Redwood City and San Mateo. The dividing line between city and country is the San Andreas Fault, the villain of the piece not just in the 1906 San Francisco Earthquake, but in dozens of others, including the one that interrupted the World Series in 1989. The twenty-mile-deep rift, named for St. Andrew, the patron saint of Scotland, runs for some six hundred miles, but among the redwoods near Portola State Park, it's possible to get out of your car and take a walk down into it and wonder why so many tract houses have been built nearby. Along the way up the Peninsula, there is plenty of evidence of what the Fault can do, including Devil's Slide, a four-hundred-foot cliff that overlooks and obviously threatens the beach at Gray Whale Cove.

SAN FRANCISCO

At Pacifica, Route One becomes a serious highway again and heads straight as a die toward San Francisco. The stretch is called the Cabrillo Highway in honor of Juan Rodriguez Cabrillo, who became the first white man to explore the California coast back in 1542. But when he sailed past, he never saw this stretch of the coast, which was shrouded in fog at the time. It wasn't until 1769 that Jose Portola pushed up overland from Monterey, and from the top of the 1,100-foot Montara Mountain saw "a large arm of the sea … [and] some mountains were made out that seemed to make an opening." The combination later became known as San Francisco Bay when the mission established there in 1776 was dedicated to St. Francis of Assisi, and the Golden Gate, named in 1846 by Captain John C. Fremont, a government explorer, who thought it would become as important as Istanbul's Golden Horn as a landfall for riches from the Orient.

The highway skirts east of Lake Merced on its way to the Golden Gate and heads up through the residential section of the city appropriately called Sunset, then across Golden Gate Park, through the Richmond District and the Presidio before reaching the bridge. But San Francisco is one of those cities that calls out to you to get off the beaten path and do some exploring. The main part of the city is off to the right, and the best way to see it from a car is by following the circular route the Convention and Visitor's Bureau calls the 49-Mile Drive. Don't let the name fool you, forty-nine is a mystical number to San Franciscans. The route is actually seventy miles long, but there are wonders to behold every foot of the way. The coastal section goes around the West side of Lake Merced and past sandy beaches and the western edge of Golden Gate Park, a thousand acres of lawns and gardens and groves of trees that cuts half-way across the city on land that was once nothing more than sand dunes. Just beyond the park are the shoreside ruins of the Sutro Baths, once a collection of six Olympic-sized swimming pools, three restaurants and more than five hundred dressing rooms, all under a magnificent stained-glass dome. The place lives on in fanciful prints and posters which can be found in the tourist shops at Cliff House, the third on the site, replacing two that burned to the ground. It's worth a stop for the view (if not for the food and souvenirs), which is a magnificent sweep of the ocean punctuated by the slightly misnamed Seal Rocks, a favorite stomping ground of the sea lions that helped make San Francisco famous. Just beyond it is Land's End, whose cliffs and seascapes are almost exactly what the whole area looked like before the hand of man arrived on the scene.

The largest woodland in the city is the 1,500-acre Presidio, a military outpost established by the Spanish in 1776 and appropriated by the United States Army seventy years later. The soldiers are still there, but the Presidio is far from anyone's stereotype of what an Army post should look like. The views of the bay alone would make anyone want to join up. And as a bonus it includes the anchorage of the Golden Gate Bridge.

It's not the longest suspension bridge in the world, but the Golden Gate is easily the most loved. It is a symbol of San Francisco itself, and there is no better way to see the city than to walk across it. The great diorama below is just as wonderful from a car, of course, but just as San Francisco is best appreciated on foot, so is the Golden Gate Bridge. Go ahead! It's an adventure you'll never forget.

THE MARIN COAST

Once across the bridge, it's a good idea to stop and look back across the Bay at the San Fransisco skyline. It's the last cityscape you'll see for quite some time on our journey. The highway winds north from the Golden Gate past some of the most beautiful landscapes God ever created. For the next four hundred miles to the Oregon border and well beyond it you can count the large towns on your fingers and the small ones are generally tucked away out of sight. People who live in some of them have even chopped down the road signs pointing in their direction. And for more than a hundred and fifty miles there isn't a single traffic light, though there are hundreds of reasons to stop.

The adventure begins at the Golden Gate National Recreation Area, a preserve that includes all the parks and beaches in San Francisco west of Fisherman's Wharf, not forgetting Alcatraz Island, which seems to contradict the term "recreation area." But most of the protected acreage is north of the bridge, where it includes twenty-two miles of Marin County oceanfront. It includes the Audubon Bird Sanctuary and Muir Woods National Monument, a grove of coast redwoods on the slopes of Mount Tamalpais, which is the winter home of millions of colorful monarch butterflies. Some of the coast redwoods in Muir Woods are more than two thousand years old and as tall as two hundred and fifty feet. The grove, which was named for the naturalist John Muir, is one of the last stands of these giants that once covered almost all of the North Coast. It very nearly disappeared itself back in 1907, when a local water company filed plans to turn the canyon into a reservoir, but it was saved by a conservationist who bought the land and donated it to the Federal Government. Since then, it has attracted more than a million visitors each year, but even if it gets crowded there is always a sense of quiet peace there.

More than three times that many people visit Point Reyes National Seashore each year, but there is plenty of room left over for herds of grazing cows on land leased by ranchers from the Park Service. It's a land of rolling, grass-covered plateaus and high bluffs overlooking the sea. But for all its beauty, the main attraction is a seismograph in the Visitor Center. The Olema Valley on the peninsula was the epicenter of the 1906 'quake that rocked San Francisco, and the west side of the San Andreas Fault jumped sixteen feet to the north. During the January migration of the gray whales, the lighthouse at the peninsula's southern tip is one of the best places to watch them swim past. But at any time of year, the best time to be there is early in the morning when the red-roofed lighthouse rises up from the mist.

A PAUSE FOR REFRESHMENT

In 1856, Colonel Agaston Haraszthy arrived from Hungary, bought a tract of land near the town of Sonoma and began planting grape vines. The Franciscans had been cultivating vineyards around their missions for nearly a century by then, but the Colonel outdid them all. Within two years he had planted more than 85,000 vines and was selling cuttings from them to his neighbors in the Sonoma Valley and across the way in Napa Valley. The industry he created has aged quite well and the thriving inland vineyards make a refreshing side trip from the coast.

It is also an opportunity to taste an important bit of California history. Exactly ten years before Haraszthy arrived, a band of gringos marched into the relatively new Spanish pueblo and took charge of the fort. They had been sent by the same John Fremont who named the Golden Gate, and who seemed ready to drop his façade of an innocent mapmaker. The Mexican General Guadelupe Vallejo was taken prisoner and Fremont triumphantly declared himself President of the California Republic. To make it official, one of his men created a flag out of a yard of homespun and a strip of red flannel. He painted a star in one corner, in honor of the Lone Star of Texas, and in the center he painted a representation of a grizzly bear. The symbolism, he said, was that "A bear stands his ground always, and as long as the stars shine we stand for a cause." He wasn't much of an artist, though, and the Spaniards decided it looked more like a pig. But they didn't object when it was run up the flagpole and they gave it their respect until the Stars and Stripes replaced it a few weeks later. Two more years passed before California officially became American territory, but as far as Sonoma was concerned that was just a formality. Vallejo didn't seem to care whose flag flew outside his window and stayed on as one of the city fathers. And when California's territorial status was confirmed, Fremont became one of its representatives in the U.S. Senate.

THE RUSSIAN COAST

The Spanish had never ventured much further north than San Francisco, but in 1835 the authorities in Mexico City ordered General Vallejo to establish an outpost on the northern frontier. He went to Petaluma first and then up to Santa Rosa, but the Indians drove him out and he moved over to Sonoma, which proved to be safer for civilization. The pueblo he built was the largest in all of California, and its plaza included a palacio for himself, another for his brother and a third for his brother-in-law. Then he made peace with the Indians and settled down for the life of a feudal prince. But it wasn't the Indians, or the Americans for that matter, that the authorities had been worried about. The Russians were out there on the coast and it was Vallejo's job to keep an eye on them. He built a watchtower and did the job with a spyglass.

He probably needn't have bothered. The Russians were having troubles of their own. They had been established for generations up at Sitka in Alaska, but it was hard to ship food and supplies to them across Siberia, and the Tsar's bureaucrats decided to move south to the California coast, where they could trade with the Spanish and the Indians for the things they needed. They got as far south as a spot within convenient, but politely remote, distance of San Francisco, where they built a settlement they named Rossiya, "Little Russia." The Spanish, unimpressed by the idea that they had come as potential customers rather than invaders, called it La Fuerte de los Rusos, "the fort of the Russians." The Americans went along with the image and called it Fort Ross.

There were fifty-nine buildings in the settlement, and it was surrounded by a stockade, but it was a working community, and proved peaceful intentions by exchanging tools and fabric for grain, vegetables and meat at the San Francisco Presidio and even traded with Vallejo himself. But before Little Russia could become a serious enterprise, the population of sea otters, their chief source of income, became dangerously low and they had to find another way to make ends meet. They tried farming, but that didn't work out, and an attempt at shipbuilding was also a dismal failure. Finally, after nearly thirty years of trying, they decided that the best thing to do was sell the place and head back to Alaska.

The buyer was a Swiss immigrant named John Sutter, who offered them $30,000, payable in yearly installments. He got all the buildings and all the livestock, including 9,000 sheep and 1,700 head of cattle, even a twenty-ton schooner, which he used to carry all the stuff to the site of New Helvetia, which later became Sacramento. A few years later gold was discovered near his relocated fort, but Sutter didn't profit from it and the Russians were forgotten in the gold rush that followed. Except for the downpayment, they never collected another dime.

The original site of their fort was forgotten, too. What little was left of Fort Ross was left to rot, and the 1906 earthquake just about finished the job. In the years since then, several of the buildings have been restored, including the stockade and a charming twin-domed Russian Orthodox chapel, which serves as an everlasting symbol of the time the Tsar's domain extended down the California Coast.

It extended down a dozen miles past the Russian River to Bodega Bay, where the village today looks more like it was transplanted from the coast of Maine than from Mother Russia. It serves as a prelude to what's ahead on the highway, because it's the site of the first steam-powered sawmill, established in 1843 on the site of the former Russian settlement. Incredibly, in spite of the dense forests along the North Coast, wood to build the early houses in San Francisco was imported from Hawaii. The Bodega Peninsula is still very much as it was when the huge granite outcrop at the tip served as a landmark for Russian ships, but the modern world came close to intruding on it back in the 1960s, when a huge hole was blasted out of the rock to build what was designed to be the largest nuclear power plant in North America. Environmentalists fought off the builders and work was stopped in 1962, after it was pointed out that the plant was going to rest on the western edge of the San Andreas Fault, a minor point the engineers had apparently overlooked. After they left, the hole eventually filled with water, creating a summer resort for ducks.

There are hundreds of monuments to environmentalist battles won and lost along the California Coast, but a few miles inland on the banks of the Russian River is one of the world's great monuments to real power, a 2,400-acre forest of virgin redwoods known as Bohemian Grove. It is the exclusive territory of San Francisco's Bohemian Club, which was originally an organization of artists and writers, actors and musicians, who entertained each other in the huge outdoor theater at the Grove. Early in its history, the club began allowing politicians and businessmen to join in the fun and, as often happens, the associate members took over. Ever since 1878, the camp on the Russian River has been the scene of the the annual "High Jinks," a revel that allows corporate chairmen to rub elbows with kings and presidents, and their cabinet members to let their hair down in the company of princes and potentates and the huddled masses from the boardrooms of multinational companies. Apart from being rich and powerful, all the revelers are men.

Those of us who, for one reason or another, are forced to be on the outside looking in have plenty of better things to look at as Route One winds up the coast from the Russian River over high ridges with long vistas of unspoiled oceanfront, and in and out of forest-filled canyons There aren't many signs of human life, and it wasn't so very long ago that the road was laced with pasture gates that motorists had to open and close every few miles. The sheep are still out there, if not in the right of way, and the beachfront, which is as wild as it has ever been, is mostly private property. Fourteen miles of the highway pass directly through Sea Ranch, a community of contemporary homes that are either awesome or awful, depending on your opinion of contemporary houses in general. It's a controversial development, but architecture isn't what the controversy is all about. When the meadows and woodlands were subdivided, back in the 1960s, conservationists began attacking it on the grounds that it would cut off public access to the beach, which as they pointed out was the property of all the people, at least below the high tide mark. The developers, who said that they had hired armed guards because their buyers were entitled to a safe environment, fought back, and the case eventually went all the way to the Supreme Court. The conservationists won their point, and four trails were built across Sea Ranch from the highway to the beach. But there is a catch. There are three parking lots serving the four footpaths, but all of them put together can only accommodate eighteen cars, so if you want to catch some rays at Sea Ranch, it's a good idea to get there first thing in the morning.

THE MENDOCINO COAST

Almost the direct opposite of the Bauhaus-inspired Sea Ranch houses, Mendocino looks more like an old New England fishing village than any other town on the California coast. It was once a lumber port, settled by loggers who went west from Maine, but its Victorian charm has turned it into an artist colony and a vacation spot. Some of the boutiques and restaurants were named by entrepreneurs who had a bad case of the cutes, but they were all careful not to disturb the character of the town that was there before they arrived. When the lumber mill closed its doors in the mid-1930s, Mendocino seemed ready to share the fate of a lot of other coastal towns, but the people who lived there decided to stay put. They could have made a better living somewhere else, but there aren't many places anywhere that are a better place to live. The result is a place where time has stood still –beautifully.

Not even the most chauvinistic boosters of other sections of the Pacific shoreline challenge Mendocino County's boast that theirs is the "Enchanted Coast." The adventure begins with the high bridge over the Albion River, and continues over high, rocky headlands with views of the sea which is almost a royal purple accented with whitecaps and sun-splashed spray as the waves break on the rocks far below. The highway winds between dark, forested hills and the ocean below, across narrow valleys and hidden coves and around the edge of dramatic cliffs. It's a challenge to drive the fifty miles of the Mendocino Coast without feeling the urge to stop and stay there forever. Even more of a challenge is deciding just where you'd like to stay. Some of the best country inns and bed and breakfast establishments in all of California dot the coast between Little River and Fort Bragg.

Among the wonders to behold on the way is the Jughandle Ecological Staircase, a good place to get a taste of the geology of the Pacific Coast. Each of the four marine terraces is separated by about a hundred feet and a hundred thousand years. The one at the top resembles the surrounding countryside, covered with pine and cypress trees, the next level down is forested with oaks and maples that give way to groves of hemlock. Each level has its own distinct growth of trees, and the one at the bottom, which the sea is still building, is a forest of dwarf trees stunted by the shallow soil. Eventually, but not any time soon, the lower terrace will be uplifted just as the other four have been. Not far away is the Mendocino Coast Botanical Garden, a fifty-acre wonderland that has examples of every kind of plant that grows along this stretch of the coast, carefully planned so that something is always in bloom there.

The preserve is at the edge of Fort Bragg, still a thriving lumber town in an area where almost all the others have either changed their ways or become ghost towns. Credit for Fort Bragg's salvation belongs to the local skunk. It is the town's lifeline and its major tourist attraction. The skunk is a railroad, built in 1855, and extending forty miles into the mountains. Its name comes from the time its steam engines were replaced by diesels and the locals began complaining about the smell. But passengers on benches fastened to the open flatcars are far more likely to be impressed by the smells of the forest. The railroad's destination is the little inland town of Willits, which in the 1880s was the headquarters of the bandit who called himself "Black Bart." He was credited with holdups of nearly thirty stagecoaches, but he didn't operate in the Wild West tradition. Bart always appeared along the road on foot, dressed in a linen duster, and treated his victims with a brand of courtesy that would make any mother proud to call him her son. When the express boxes he took were found after he himself had melted into the forest, they always contained an original poem signed "Black Bart, Po8." He met his downfall when he dropped a handkerchief during one of his robberies. The laundry mark led detectives to San Francisco, where Bart turned out to be a respectable and quite successful mining engineer who frequently took business trips up north into the mountains, and seems to have done some moonlighting on the way. He paid for his crimes with a two-year stay at San Quentin Prison, another landmark along the California Coast.

THE REDWOOD HIGHWAY

Above Fort Bragg, the highway passes through sand dunes, replacing the rocky coast it has followed for so long. Then, suddenly, rugged mountains block the way and the road is forced to turn abruptly inland. This is the King Range; mountains that rise up as high as four thousand feet in a mile or two. Almost no roads of any description penetrate them, but the route around them, though it is out of sight of fifty-five miles of coastline, cuts through the heart of California's redwood empire.

The road has passed through several groves of redwood beginning as far south as Monterey. But they were just a preview of what lies ahead. The trees further north are taller, the tallest on earth, in fact. The groves are more dense and the silence in the deep shade is the most profound of any spot in the world.

Some of these trees have been thriving in the coastal fog for two thousand years, but even they are relative newcomers in a family that fossil evidence suggests has been in the world for some 160 million years, once ranging over the whole Northern hemisphere. The great glaciers destroyed nearly all of them, except for a thirty-mile-wide belt extending 450 miles along the California coast. Their scientific name is Sequoia Sempervirens, not to be confused with their distant relative, Sequoia Gigantea, that lives in the Sierras. Both were named for the Cherokee Chief Sequoyah, who created an alphabet for his people and taught them to read and write. Redwoods grow taller than Sequoias, but the Sequoias are more massive. Both seemed to be hellbent for extinction until the turn of the century, when forests and groves of both species were declared off-limits to loggers. The wood of the Sequoia is brittle, and the loggers gave up easily. But, as John Muir pointed out, "As lumber, the coast redwoods were too good to live." Its wood is straight-grained, it doesn't shrink, it resists decay and, best of all, it is easy to cut. The battle between the woodsmen and the conservationists over the redwoods doesn't show any of stopping.

The cutting of redwoods began back in the late 1820s and is still going on. The effort to save them is still going on, too, but since 1902, when the first redwood park was established south of San Francisco, only about two-and-a-half percent of the original trees have been protected. And ninety-seven percent of all the redwoods left in the world are on the 387-mile stretch of Route 101 known as the Redwood Highway.

The road cuts right through the middle of Richardson Grove State Park, one of the oldest and best-developed of the redwood preserves. And not far north of it, a thirty-three-mile alternate route known as the Avenue of the Giants runs through the thick groves of Humboldt Redwoods State Park and the Founder's Grove, dedicated to the Save The Redwoods League, which has been responsible for preserving 150,000 acres of trees. The road also passes near the Rockefeller Grove, which includes a 359-foot giant thought to be the tallest in the world until an even taller one was discovered nearby in the 1960s.

The highway gets its sea views back when it reaches Humboldt Bay, north of Cape Mendocino, the westernmost point of land in the Continental United States. It is also near Ferndale, a Victorian-style town where the clock seems to have stopped at 1870. There is more Victoriana a few miles north at Eureka, the biggest town on California's North Coast, with a population of about 25,000. It has more than one hundred Victorian houses, including the famous Carson Mansion, a wedding cake of gothic turrets built in the 1880s by a lumber millionaire with a strong desire to be noticed.

Like a dramatic ending to a symphony, the California portion of the coast comes to an end at Redwood National Park, covering some forty miles of shoreline and encompassing three state parks: Jedediah Smith Redwoods, Del Norte Coast Redwoods and Prairie Creek Redwoods. The best way to enjoy the park is to pick a day in the late spring, when the rhododendrons are in bloom, and make sure it's also a foggy day when the sunlight is filtered and sends random motes of light to the forest floor. The 110,000-acre park was dedicated in 1968 by President Lyndon Johnson and his wife Lady Bird, who was one of the prime movers in its creation and is the namesake of one of its loveliest groves. Naturally, the logging interests fought the idea for years, and by the time the government acquired the final forty thousand acres, the trees had been cut from all but ten thousand of them. To stop the erosion that had already begun, the new owners planted nearly a million new trees that will reach maturity in a thousand years or so. It made Redwood the most expensive creation in the National Park system. But the loss of any more of those magnificent trees to make picnic tables and patios would have been an expense bordering on the unbearable.

THE OREGON COAST

The three hundred and sixty-mile coast from the California line to the Columbia River often looks so much like the West Coast of Ireland that it's tempting to put an apostrophe after the "O" in Oregon. High cliffs run close to the sea in many places, and in the State's early years the only way to get up and down the coast was on the beach itself, and then only when the tide was out. Many of the communities there were established as logging towns and fishing villages with no access except by water. People got so used to the idea that when construction began on a coastal highway in 1921, they began taking bets that it would never be finished because they had long since decided that such a thing must be impossible. It took more than ten years to prove them wrong, and even then some of the rivers still had to be crossed on ferries. Bridges, many of them quite beautiful, have solved that problem. And as a means of protecting the coast from the overdevelopment the highway could bring, the State of Oregon has thoughtfully set aside State Parks every few miles all the way up the coast.

The state line changes the designation of North Coast, which is what Californians call everything above San Francisco, to South Coast to reflect a different point of view on the part of the Oregonians. Oddly, the weather seems to conspire to make it feel more like the south. Between the border and the town of Brookings, the coastal plain turns eastward, giving the area a southern exposure that makes it the warmest spot in all of Oregon in the winter months and, because of the sea breezes, the summer temperature doesn't vary much, either. The result is that flowers bloom in Brookings all year round. If the locals ever get the idea to strew flowers in the path of visitors, though, chances are good that they will be Easter lilies. More than ninety percent of all the white lilies that are sold by America's florists originated on this short stretch of the Oregon Coast.

Brookings also has a large commercial fishing fleet, which serves as a preview of what to expect on the way north. It also serves as a reminder to take along a fishing pole or at least a healthy appetite for seafood. Any big ones that get away will probably turn up as the catch of the day in one of those great restaurants up ahead.

Until quite recently the highway out of town went up over the mountains and out of sight of the sea, but now it is possible to drive near the beaches and stop to contemplate the offshore rock formations, and possibly spot a pod of whales swimming past. The sand on the beaches is black in spite of the fact that the next major town is called Gold Beach. Back in 1852 gold was discovered upstream on the Rogue River, and some smart prospectors decided that the wild river was carrying its riches off to sea and set up placer mines on the beach to catch it at the river's mouth. They washed a lot of sand, but didn't find much gold in it, and finally gave up after heavy flood tides carried most of the sand and any gold it may have contained out to sea. After the highway reached the town it became a resort whose main attraction is the fifty-two-mile lower stretch of the river, which is not only spectacularly beautiful, but offers adventure in the form of white water rafting and, of course, fishing.

Cruises on the Coquille River at Bandon are a bit gentler, and there is even a sternwheel steamboat to add to the fun. Unlike her woodburning predecessors that used to send showers of sparks from their smokestacks, she's powered by less combustible engines and is considered a solid citizen in a town that has good reason to worry about such things. Bandon was founded in 1873 by Lord George Bennett, an Irish peer who named it for his hometown in County Cork. It's one of those spots along the South Coast that looks a lot like Ireland, but Lord Bennett heightened the effect by importing furze bushes, the Irish relative of the gorse, which he found beautiful and which were also practical as a means of anchoring the sand dunes. But its yellow flowers are filled with highly flammable oil, and when a 1936 forest fire spread to the dunes the bushes began exploding and raining fire into the streets of the town. People trying to escape the flames by car found their tires melted to the pavement, and even the green grass on shore caught fire. When the flames burned themselves out, more than five hundred buildings had vanished, and though more than 2,000 people were evacuated on coast guard boats, sixteen died and it looked very much as though Bandon itself had died along with them. It was all eventually rebuilt, but the furze bushes are still thriving, so it's a good idea to take "No Smoking" signs seriously.

The dunes Lord Bennett was trying to control take over completely above the mountains that once made the South Coast so isolated, and the shoreline changes completely north of Bandon. The coastal plain extends much further inland, creating extensive wetlands, and the general appearance of the shore for the next seventy-five miles is more like the Atlantic Coast than the Pacific.

At first glance, the huge bridge that carries the highway across Coos Bay might make it seem like the more industrialized sections of the Atlantic Seaboard, and though it passes one of the most heavily populated parts of Oregon and the largest lumber port in the world, the bay itself is one of the State's treasures, and one of the best places on the coast to take your shoes off and poke around for clams. The other side of the bridge marks the southern boundary of Oregon Dunes National Recreation Area, a forty-mile swath of sand dunes as much as seven hundred feet high and a mile long. It is one of the very few government-controlled reserves that allows off-road vehicles, but in places where the dune buggies haven't chewed up the landscape, it is a perfect place for hiking, beachcombing, fishing and birdwatching, as well as for contemplating the forces of wind, sand and water.

After crossing the charming Art Deco bridge over the Siuslaw River at Florence, the coastline changes again as high mountains once more hug the shore, and the highway winds around them over high bridges and even through a tunnel at a point appropriately called Devil's Elbow. There are places where the sea crashes through caves, creating spectacular waterspouts, and near some of them the highway is perpetually wet. Usually called the Central Coast, the seventy-five-mile stretch north to Devil's Lake is a favorite among romantics who enjoy watching wild winter storms. They are never disappointed, and there are plenty of places along the way where they can sit by a roaring fire with a brandy in hand listening to the wind rattling the windows.

The highway turns inland at Neskowin to skirt the capes up ahead and the large Tillamook Bay. This is dairy country, with more cows than people, and one of the biggest cheese-producing counties in America. The heavy rain produces unusually thick grass, which in turn produces unusually rich milk. A century ago most of it was turned into butter, but a capricious sandbar at the mouth of the harbor often delayed ships so long that the butter was rancid before it could be shipped out. The solution was to turn the milk into cheese, which is more forgiving of delays, and these days the Tillamook dairy farmers (who prefer to be called ranchers out here) ship nearly fifty million pounds of cheese a year. But they ship it by truck and rail rather than in the holds of ships.

Trucks heading north twist up over Neahkahine Mountain, a 1,795-ft. headland that was one of the spots skeptics said the highway could never pass. But dynamite and patience proved them wrong, and the result is a driving adventure with beautiful scenic turnouts along the way. Some folks say you could see all the way to China from up there if the fog would lift. They're probably wrong, but you can see the Clatsop Prairie up to the north, the beginning of what local boosters call the Sunset Empire.

The beach is wide here and the inland mountains impressive. But the sun isn't always cooperative in splashing the sea with color when it sets. It rains a lot in this part of the Pacific Northwest and in the summer the fog doesn't let up for days on end. People who live here get used to it, some even seem to like it, and even little children can recite weather bureau statistics that it rains 160 days a year, mostly when they're in school anyway, but that there are 200 days a year when it doesn't rain at all. So there.

This is the territory that was the end of the trail for the Lewis and Clark expedition back in 1805 and where they spent the winter resting up for the trip back to St. Louis. They camped on the banks of the Columbia River for 106 days, only twelve of which were not rainy. But that didn't stop people from following them. Four years after they left, John Jacob Astor's minions established a fur trading post at Astoria, which makes it the oldest American settlement west of the Mississippi. When the British took control of it a year later, the Astorians weren't at all happy to leave, and when pioneer families began establishing their homes there a few years later they never looked back.

Until 1966, the highway along the Pacific Coast didn't cross the Columbia River and it was necessary to catch a ferry to get across the state line. The Astoria-Megler Bridge put the ferry out of business, and though it is only a little more than four miles long, it rises almost two hundred feet above the river for a gull's-eye view of the estuary that Lewis and Clark's men were convinced was the ocean itself.

THE WASHINGTON COAST

The first landfall on the north bank of the Columbia is Cape Disappointment, but don't let the name fool you. It's a beautiful spot and one of the last of the dramatic coast headlands that make Oregon so spectacular. It got its name from the British explorer, John Meares, who tried to cross the sandbar in 1792 and gave it up as impossible. Much less disappointing was the attempt by the American John Gray, who made it across a few weeks later and named the river for his ship, Columbia, which was the first American vessel to sail around the world and much, much later became the namesake of an American space shuttle.

But that sandbar never stopped disappointing mariners, many of whom went down with their ships trying to get across it. And in spite of the jetty that was built to control it, and the lighthouse that marks it, sailing into the mouth of the Columbia is still a tricky business. Because of it, ship owners opted to use the inland harbors along Puget Sound and without it, Seattle might still be a small town.

A long, sandy peninsula extends for twenty-eight miles north of the cape, separating the sea from Wallapa Bay and, as was the case at Oregon's southern tip, the Chamber of Commerce serving the seven little towns along the shore claims it is the warmest spot on the Washington Coast. As proof they point to the cranberry bogs that thrive there, producing more than three million pounds of red berries a year. Oysters seem to like it there, too. They are responsible for eighteen million dollars a year for the local economy.

Wallapa Bay and Grays Harbor a few miles north, along with the Quinault Indian Reservation, force the coastal highway inland all the way up to the Olympic Mountains. But the ocean is never more than thirty miles away and it's easy to run out to Westport for whale-watching or to Ocean Shores for surf casting.

On the other hand, it's possible to see the Olympic Mountains ahead in the distance, and their call is irresistible. The highway has passed around and through mountains almost all the way from Mexico, but nothing near the coast compares with the Olympics. Not many mountains anywhere do.

They are a collection of hundreds of jagged peaks, the most rugged in the American West, rising from five-thousand to nearly eight-thousand feet above sea level, which is only a few miles away. Most of them are covered with snow that never melts, and there are more than fifty glaciers on their slopes. But there is much more to the Olympic Peninsula than awe-inspiring mountains. More than 142 inches of rain fall on the ocean side each year and over 200 inches of snow fall in the winter, creating an unusual coniferous rainforest, the only temperate jungle in America, with huge spruce, fir, cedar and bigleaf maples festooned with moss and vines rising up from a spongy, moss-covered forest floor. It overlooks nearly fifty miles of unspoiled seacoast with long stretches of beach, where it is possible to walk for miles with only seals and seagulls for company.

The highway, which winds out of sight of the ocean for all but about a hundred miles in Washington, turns inland again through the Olympic National Forest, but a side trip up to Neah Bay at the edge of the Makah Indian Reservation makes that seem like a blessing. Just beyond is Cape Flattery, the northwestern edge of the Continental United States. Because it is served by a gravel road rather than a paved highway, not many people go there. But those who do can stand on the edge of a hundred-foot cliff and let their imagination soar. It's a mysterious place, surrounded by a thick forest of spruces. It is often shrouded in fog and, because the water is so deep, the waves don't usually crash against the rocks, but rather move in and out of the caves below, making sounds that are more like breathing than roaring.

Vancouver Island is less than twenty miles away to the north, but the next landfall to the west is the Kuril Islands, and they lie across nearly five thousand miles of open water. The highway that made it possible to reach this point from Baja California loops around the top of the peninsula and down along the Hood Canal on its way to Olympia. It's a beautiful trip, but then again, you might be tempted to stay at Cape Flattery forever. It's that kind of place. The Makah Indians have been living there for twenty-five thousand years and if it seems a bit removed from civilization, they don't seem to care.

Previous page and left: wave- and wind-swept driftwood on Rialto Beach, (above) silken sands at Kalaloch and (overleaf) La Push Beach, all of which lie within Olympic National Park, Washington. These beaches are superb for beachcombing, their tide pools remain full of life, and not only birds and sea lions visit the shore – bears and wildcats have been known to wander here. La Push is one of the last wilderness beaches in the conterminous United States. Above left: frolicking in the surf at Grayland Beach State Park on the southern Washington coast.

Above: the picturesque harbor at Tokeland, a town on the Washington coast established in the nineteenth century and named after a local Indian chief. The Shoalwater Indians, who lived on the strip of land nearby known as Toke Point, were wiped out, like so many native tribes, by smallpox carried to the region by white settlers. Tokeland is largely unspoilt and retains a nineteenth-century atmosphere. Above right: South Bend oyster shells – the mill town of South Bend on Willapa Bay boasts a fully automated oyster-processing plant. Willapa (right), its sister town, is equally involved in the oyster trade, while to the south, the Pacific town of Ilwaco (overleaf) is devoted to sea fishing, receiving many seasonal visitors eager to catch halibut, tuna and sturgeon.

Above and right: the Trans Columbia Bridge, which connects Astoria in Oregon with Megler in Washington across the mighty Columbia River. Situated in the extreme northwestern tip of Oregon, Astoria has always been connected with the development of the Columbia; large ships leave here bound for the Far East with cargoes of wood and wheat harvested from the fertile valleys of this river. Passage for such vessels was interrupted in a major way after the eruption of Mount St. Helens because the river was so full of volcanic debris that it had to be dredged. Above right: the lightship Columbia, *which served as a visual aid for ships crossing the Columbia Bar from 1950 to 1980. Overleaf: Cannon Beach stretching away south from Ecola State Park near Seaside.*

The Oregon coast is one of the most spectacularly beautiful in all of North America and, not surprisingly, it attracts artists of all descriptions. Cannon Beach (left), in the north, has become, in the words of one guide, a "coastal cultural milieu," and can boast numerous art galleries as well as a flourishing theater and the Haystack Program of the Arts, a major summer event that includes classes in music, photography, sculpture and painting. The town received its unusual name from a cannon that was washed ashore here in 1846. Cannon Beach looks out upon a huge offshore monolith known, rather unromantically, as Haystack Rock (overleaf). Today this is a bird sanctuary.

Cannon Beach seen from the south, as mist rolls in with the tide across surf-trawled sand. The beaches of north Oregon are set with some of the purest, most unpolluted tidal pools in the country; teeming with color and life. Alongside Dungeness crabs, goose barnacles, mussels and a garden of coral, the patient searcher can find a world populated by blood-red starfish, sapphire blue anemones, pincushion-like sea urchins, inquisitive copper rockfish, sun stars and giant green anemones that resemble chrysanthemums. Such a heritage is recognized as priceless by the people of Oregon: over sixty state parks have been established along this 350-mile-long coast — indeed, there are more parks than towns.

Facing page: the superb coast that is the highlight of Oswald West State Park – 2,562 acres that lie five miles north of Manzanita on the U.S. Highway 101 in Oregon. This park, Tolovona Beach Wayside (above), which lies just south of Cannon Beach, and Netarts Bay (overleaf), which forms part of Cape Lookout State Park, combine to make up one of the most extensive park systems of the Western States. Set aside for recreation, conservation, for their scenic value or historical significance, these areas are popular throughout the year. The beaches are, mostly, in their natural state – this and their convenient proximity to the highway make them irresistible.

Right: nineteenth-century Yaquina Light, which stands in the north of Yaquina Bay, a state park on Highway 101. The light, which is furnished in period and open to visitors, is reputedly haunted, having been the site of a mysterious murder. Its summer caretaker is happy to point out what appear to be blood stains at the bottom of the light's spiral staircase – though they might equally well be rust stains from an aged dripping pipe, nobody knows for certain. Overleaf: Yaquina Bay Bridge, a familiar landmark in Newport, the largest port on the central Oregon coast. Settled in 1855 as a fishing village, today the city is the home of the Oregon State University's Marine Science Center. It also serves the lumber industries of inland Oregon and is the hub of the Dungeness crab industry.

Above: Heceta Head Light, which was built north of Florence in southern Oregon in 1894. The light bears Oregon's most powerful beacon, having a one-million-candlepower beam. Near the light can be found a famous colony of Steller's sea lions (above left), which breed beside the sea in a huge cavern some 125 feet in height. This is the only place on the American mainland where these wild sea lions breed; they can be seen here in spring and summer on the ledges outside the cave in herds dominated by huge sea lion bulls. Also near Heceta Head can be found over 2,000 Brandt cormorants (left); in the breeding season this is the world's largest colony of these birds.

The view south along Heceta Beach towards
Darlingtonia Botanical Wayside and the
nineteenth-century fishing town of Florence,
which is noted for its rhododendrons: a
Rhododendron Festival takes place there in May.
Florence was once home to the Siuslaw, an
Indian tribe which, in 1855, gave up two-and-a-
half million acres of its land to the Federal
government. Much of that land is now part of
the Siuslaw National Forest, an extensive area of
some 628,000 acres which borders the sea from
North Bend to Cape Lookout and includes sea
cliffs a thousand feet high.

Above: the immaculate landscaped gardens that make Shore Acres State Park (overleaf) one of the loveliest state parks in Oregon. The park, which lies off Route 101 southwest of Coos Bay, was once the estate of Louis J. Simpson, the son of the lumber baron Captain Asa M. Simpson. It is said that the Captain was not impressed by his son's choice of building site – on sailing past the headland at Cape Arago and spying the house being built, he enquired as to what fool it was that had chosen such a place. Ultimately it would seem that the site was unlucky – the house burned down twice and Louis, failing in business, was obliged to give all over to the state in 1934. Above right: the Jessie M. Honeyman Memorial State Park, part of the Oregon Dunes National Recreation Area (right), which preserves dunes left after a glacial retreat some 15,000 years ago.

Above: a solitary monolith stands before a small forest of bleached driftwood on the beach of Cape Blanco State Park, Oregon. This park, which comprises over 1,800 acres and lies nine miles north of Port Orford off U.S. Highway 101, includes the most western point in the contiguous United States. Horse riding, camping and hiking are available here, though perhaps the most relaxing pursuit simply involves looking for beautiful driftwood along the shore. Above right: dramatic rock forms on a secluded beach in Pistol River State Park which, like those at Cape Sebastion State Park (right), might seem to the fanciful like Oregon's teeth bared against the might of the sea.

Right: an unusual black sand beach lies at the
head of a cove in Samuel H. Boardman State
Park. Named for the founder of Oregon's state
park system, this ten-mile-long park lies six
miles to the north of the town of Brookings on
U.S. Highway 101. It is famous for the
spectacular beauty of its ocean views. Overleaf:
sunset on the beach of Harris Beach State Park
reduces seabirds and people to silhouettes. Harris
Beach is also on Highway 101, only two miles
north of Brookings and therefore the most
southerly of all Oregon's coastal state parks. Its
scenic rock cliffs along the ocean are one of its
main attractions. Brookings, situated close to the
Californian state border, is the nation's major
producer of Easter lily and daffodil bulbs.

A forest of masts belonging to both pleasure craft and fishing boats congregate in Brookings harbor. Oregon's most southwesterly town, Brookings is a commercial fishing port, processing salmon, tuna, shrimp, crab and rock fish, while also being a major sportfishing center. Here the deep-sea fishing and year-round freshwater fishing is particularly good: the Chetco River, flowing out of the mountains just south of Brookings, has salmon, steelhead and cutthroat trout runs sufficient to occupy the most devoted angler. Brookings also holds an intriguing annual festival for those happy to explore the shoreline for a good catch – the Driftwood Show in April attracts connoisseur beachcombers from miles around.

Above: a view from Klamath Overlook, a place to pause along U.S. Highway 101 near the town of the same name in Northern California. The Klamath River is renowned as a great angling stream, indeed, it is one of the finest of its kind in the state, drawing fishermen from all over eager to catch steelhead trout and salmon. Above the Del Norte County line a two-mile-long line of campers and other recreational vehicles (facing page) are parked along the beach bordering U.S. 101 near the mouth of the Klamath during the fishing season, each one bearing witness to the excellence of the sport here. Overleaf: mighty redwoods peek through a fog bank to greet the dawn as it breaks over Redwood National Park.

Left: Fern Canyon, Prairie Creek State Park, a place of lush vegetation in Northern California, where heavy rainfall and a sheltered environment have encouraged the growth of some of the world's tallest trees, redwoods. The best of these are to be found in Redwood National Park, which stretches along the Californian coast for forty miles from Crescent City to Orick, afterwards turning inland to follow Redwood Creek, where the six tallest trees in the world grow. This famous park was established by President Johnson in 1968 to consolidate the forested parts of the Northern Californian coastline under federal jurisdiction; a stand of trees in the park was named Lady Bird Johnson Grove (overleaf) in honor of the President's popular wife.

Above left: the diminutive light at Trinidad Head: since the cliff upon which it is built is so high, the light tower itself needs no more height. Constructed in 1871, the light was designed to serve coastal shipping and still does so today. Trinidad Head lies to the north of the city of Eureka (above), the largest city in California north of Sacramento. Eureka was founded in 1850 and its unusual name is thought to relate to the gold rush that established the town. Today, the gold having all been found, Eureka centers around a thriving lumbering industry, though its citizens find plenty of time for recreation at Woodly Island Marina (left) on the outskirts of the city.

Highway 101 comes very close to the sea at Elk Creek (right), south of Mendocino. Close to this part of the Californian coast (overleaf) and bordering the highway lies the sizeable state park of Van Damme. Here camping, hiking, beachcombing and fishing are possible, but most visitors come to marvel at the park's pygmy forest of cypress and Bolander pines. These trees' development has been stunted by their having to grow in a shallow sill leached of essential nutrients by heavy rains and by having a hardpan subsoil resistant to root penetration. Since such soils occur in patches, these trees appear alongside normal-sized ones as nature's version of bonsai trees.

An aerial view of Northern California's Point Reyes Light (above) clearly shows the dramatic isolation of its position. Point Reyes, a distinctively shaped peninsula, has been designated in its entirety as a National Seashore, encompassing an extensive forest, as well as miles of broad beaches. The preserve's eastern edge is clearly defined by the San Andreas Fault – after this point, the Fault disappears beneath the Pacific Ocean. Above right: a view from Salt Point, California, which lies north of Point Reyes and is part of a state park, and (right) Bodega Bay Harbor, where freshly caught albacore can be bought directly from local fishermen.

Californian poppies, the state flower, bloom in cheerful array as the tide goes out along the Sonoma coast. The grazing land that edges this coast is so valuable as real estate that those who farm it are known as "boutique farmers," a reference to the fact that they don't really have to farm, since they could make more by selling the land to developers than they ever will in a lifetime of cultivating it.

Left: San Francisco-Oakland Bay Bridge and (overleaf) the Golden Gate Bridge, which is more than three miles long and stands as the third longest suspension bridge in the world. On May 27th, 1987, the city celebrated the bridge's fiftieth anniversary by closing it to cars, reserving it for pedestrians. In one day over 800,000 people paid homage to the Golden Gate Bridge, one of the wonders of the West Coast, by crossing it – and the central span sagged more than two feet under the weight.

State Highway 1 skirts Gray Whale Cove Beach, part of a state beach just south of San Francisco near Montara. As the name suggests, gray whales have often been sighted off the coast at this point; indeed, these mammals are visible all along the Californian coast through the winter. This is the time that the whales migrate from Alaska to the warm waters of Baja California to give birth to their young, making the return journey in the spring. Whale-watchers with binoculars comb the horizon from the cliffs in hope of seeing a pod and, with luck, the little, two-foot-high spout that indicates the presence of a calf among them.

Above: Carmel River State Beach, just one of the attractions of Carmel, a little village on the Northern Californian coast famous for its genteel atmosphere, unusual shops, lack of streetlights, stoplights, parking meters, sidewalks or curbs. Equally popular with visitors is Fisherman's Wharf (above right) in Monterey, a historic town that lies to the north of Carmel. The Wharf is lined with restaurants, shops and fresh fish markets, while below it sea lions can be spied swimming among the pilings, hopeful for some spare fish. Right: flowers spread a natural carpet across Lovers' Point in Pacific Grove, California. The Grove lies at the northernmost tip of the Monterey Peninsula and during the Depression was home to a then poverty-stricken John Steinbeck.

Below: the famous lone pine cypress that stands defiant on an outcrop of rock at Midway Point, also known as Sunset Point, near Monterey, Northern California. The tree is supported by wires secured to the rock face, an attempt to ensure that the cypress doesn't succumb to the force of the prevailing Pacific winds. Much photographed, especially at sunset, the tree is famous nationwide as a symbol of this coast's rugged beauty. Right: the rock formations known as the Pinnacles, (below right) Sea Lion Cove and (overleaf) a view towards Monterey Cypress Grove, all highlights of Point Lobos State Reserve, south of Monterey. Stretching for six miles along Highway State 1, the reserve claims, justifiably, to be one of the most beautiful spots on the Californian coast.

Left: California's Bixby Creek slips down to the sea, dwarfed by the famous span of Bixby Bridge, which carries State Highway 1,260 feet above the canyon the creek has carved. The Pacific Coast Highway has frequently been closed along its stretch here due to severe landslides: in 1983 the route became impassable for over a year, so extensive was the damage during the spring storms. This is one of the world's most spectacular drives; the road skirts precipitous cliff edges for many miles, often shrouded in fog, though when this clears, stretches of unspoilt, cream-colored sands can be seen from the car. Overleaf: Point Sur. Big Sur's dramatic coastline, which runs from San Simeon to Carmel, California, rises almost vertically from the Pacific Ocean into the gold and green Santa Lucia mountains.

The narrow, twisting stretch of State Highway 1 between Hearst Castle at San Simeon and the Monterey Peninsula, California, was built between the wars by convict labor. It travels back and forth from sea level to 1,000 feet within a mile along the Big Sur coastline, skirting Limekiln Beach (left), Julia Pfeiffer Burns State Park (above) and the Carmel Highlands (above left). A number of inns and campgrounds can be found now along the route, but in all the road is not much changed since the thirties – there are no billboards or streetlights and there is still a sense that the traveler is moving through a wild country. Overleaf: the Greek-look swimming pool at San Simeon, once the eyrie of newspaper tycoon William Randolph Hearst.

Above: the Santa Barbara shore, fringed with palms. Known as the Cannes of the California Riviera, Santa Barbara is comprised largely of houses that are low, whitewashed, red-tiled and graceful, a style imposed by the threat of earthquakes combined with a widespread affection for Spanish architecture, which lends the city a gentle, relaxed and sophisticated air. It is said that even the poor would rather be poor in Santa Barbara than rich anywhere else! Right: Santa Monica, a popular ocean resort bounded by Los Angeles on three sides and by the Pacific on the fourth. Above right: expensive status symbols: elegant Malibu beach houses. Many of these are owned by the rich and famous who have formed the private Malibu Beach Colony, wherein they enjoy the town's wild surf and secluded beaches.

Below and overleaf: a wide expanse of sand forms the fringe of Pacific Palisades, a select suburb of Los Angeles that has been home to Ronald Reagan, Steven Speilberg and Sylvester Stallone, among others of the smart set. Right: evening shadows on Newport Beach, a town on the Pacific Coast Highway south of Los Angeles. From here is organized the annual Christmas Boat Parade, the Bathtub Regatta and the start of the race from Newport to Ensenada, Mexico. Newport Beach is an extremely popular vacation center and the variety of its shops, restaurants and sea- and beach-based events ensure the visitor much to see and do. Below right: the **Queen Mary,** *one of Long Beach's most popular attractions. Once a prestigious cruise liner that crossed the Atlantic 1,001 times, today this 81,000-ton vessel has a permanent berth in Long Beach where visitors can view the ship's interior and wonder at its luxury and glamor.*

Above left: a beach hut silhouetted by the sun in Santa Monica. Once Santa Monica was a day's stagecoach ride from Los Angeles, today it takes only thirty minutes on the freeway to reach the downtown area. Above and overleaf: the Hotel del Coronado in San Diego (left), the second largest city in California, which spreads over twenty square miles. The Hotel del Coronado has stood on the Coronado peninsula since 1888; it was host to the author Henry James in 1905 and has welcomed numerous notable personalities since. James wrote that he wished to stay awake to listen to the sound of the sea, audible from the hotel's bedrooms. The first Californian mission, San Diego de Alcalá, was founded in this area in 1769, and the city was named after it. San Diego is home to the most extensive naval air station on the west coast and in the harbor it is possible to see the largest Navy fleet of the continental United States. The city also boasts the country's biggest zoo.

Below: stratified rock rears up from the waves at Cabrillo National Monument, Point Loma, which overlooks San Diego. The monument marks the place where the Portuguese explorer Juan Rodriguez Cabrillo discovered the point and upper California in September, 1542. His sighting of this land, during a fierce autumn storm, was the first contact by a white man with California. Left: select beach houses front the Pacific coast at Bird Rock, San Diego, not far from Sunset Cliffs (below left), so named for the way their colors vary according to the time of day. Overleaf: warm, clear seas and wildflowers at La Jolla, north of San Diego, a center of research for Scripps Institution of Oceanography and the Salk Institute for Biological Studies, as well as a vacation resort since the nineteenth century.

The Pacific Coast Highway leaves California at San Diego, entering Mexico at Tijuana. Facing page, above and overleaf: Cabo San Lucas, a major resort which lies on the tip of Mexico's Baja Peninsula. Here, at Land's End (facing page), the Sea of Cortés and the Pacific meet: the resulting waves are spectacular, while the waters are excellent for deep-sea fishing. Top: La Paz, the capital of Baja Sur and once a world-renowned pearl fishing center, whose produce can be found in many European crown jewels. Today La Paz is as tranquil as its name suggests, retaining its provincial air despite development. Following page: a view from the Pacific Highway.

125

INDEX